SWORDFISH

A Buddy Book by
Deborah Coldiron

ABDO
Publishing Company

UNDERWATER WORLD

VISIT US AT
www.abdopublishing.com

Published by ABDO Publishing Company, 8000 West 78th Street, Edina, Minnesota 55439.

Copyright © 2008 by Abdo Consulting Group, Inc. International copyrights reserved in all countries. No part of this book may be reproduced in any form without written permission from the publisher. Buddy Books™ is a trademark and logo of ABDO Publishing Company.

Printed in the United States.

Coordinating Series Editor: Sarah Tieck
Contributing Editor: Michael P. Goecke
Graphic Design: Deborah Coldiron
Cover Photograph: ImageMix
Interior Photographs/Illustrations: Clipart.com (pages 9, 15, 17, 28); Corbis (page 11, 13), Minden Pictures: Fred Bavendam (pages 21, 25), Norbert Wu (pages 7); Ocean Images: John Ashley (page 19); Photos.com (pages 5, 19, 23, 29, 30); Jeff Rotman Photography (pages 18, 27); SeaPics.com Marine Wildlife Photography (page 18)

Library of Congress Cataloging-in-Publication Data

Coldiron, Deborah.
    Swordfish / Deborah Coldiron.
       p. cm. — (Underwater World)
    Includes index.
    ISBN 978-1-59928-820-8
    1. Swordfish—Juvenile literature. I. Title.

    QL638.X5C56 2007
    597.78—dc22

                                   2007016262

Table Of Contents

The World Of Swordfish

Every living creature needs water. Some animals not only need water, they live in it, too.

Scientists have found more than 250,000 kinds of plants and animals living underwater. And, they believe there could be one million more! The swordfish is one animal that makes its home in this underwater world.

Seventy percent of Earth's surface is covered in water.

Swordfish are fast, scaleless fish with long, swordlike bills. They can grow up to 15 feet (5 m) long. Some weigh as much as 1,000 pounds (450 kg)!

Swordfish are found in **tropical** and **temperate** oceans all over the world. They are often seen in areas where large **currents** meet.

FAST FACTS

Swordfish are migratory. They move to warmer waters in winter and cooler waters in summer.

Swordfish bodies are built for speed. And, these fish can travel great distances in the ocean.

Meet And Greet

There is only one **species** of swordfish in the entire world! It is called *Xiphias gladius*. *Gladius* is a Latin word that means "sword."

The swordfish is known for its long, pointed bill. It uses this to slash prey. But a swordfish bill is also flat. So, a swordfish is sometimes called a broadbill.

The Body Of A Swordfish

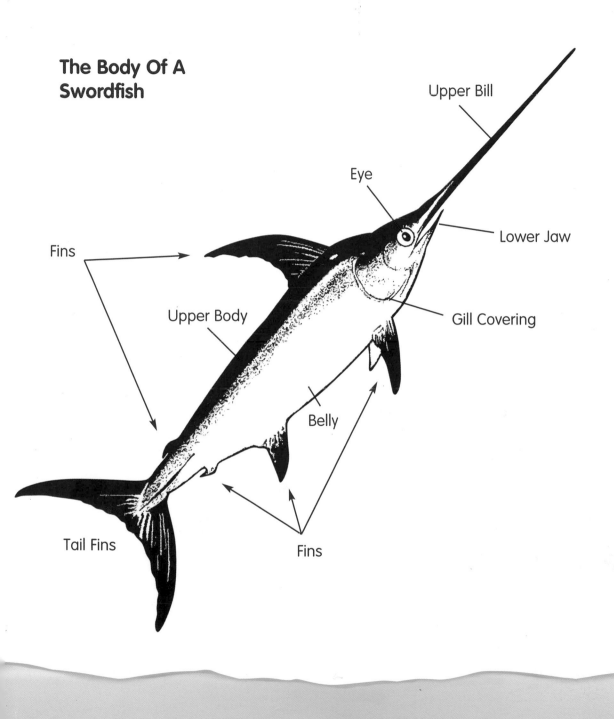

Upper Bill

Eye

Lower Jaw

Fins

Upper Body

Gill Covering

Belly

Tail Fins

Fins

The swordfish's bottom jaw is as pointy and sharp as its upper bill. But, the bottom jaw is much shorter.

Adult swordfish have no teeth. So, they swallow food whole.

Swordfish have dark skin on their backs. This skin may be brown, blue, gray, or purple. Swordfish bellies may be white or light gray.

Dark And Light

Many ocean fish have dark skin on their backs and pale bellies. When seen from above, fish with dark backs blend into the ocean's darkness. When seen from below, pale skin blends in with the sunlit surface.

This color combination helps these fish move through water unnoticed. Their skin colors help protect them from predators. These colors also allow the fish to hide while hunting prey.

Sharks have dark backs and pale bellies. So do rays, dolphins, and many other ocean animals.

Cold-Blooded Creature

Like other fish, swordfish are cold-blooded animals. Their body temperature stays just a bit higher than the temperature of the water around them.

Amphibians, such as frogs, are also cold-blooded. So are **invertebrates**, such as octopuses.

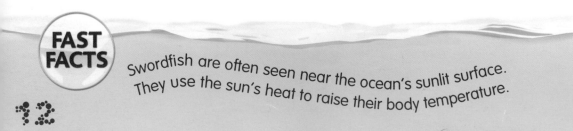

FAST FACTS

Swordfish are often seen near the ocean's sunlit surface. They use the sun's heat to raise their body temperature.

Unlike most cold-blooded creatures, swordfish have special heat organs near the eyes. These warm their eyes and brain. Scientists believe this helps swordfish see as they hunt in cold waters.

Mako sharks (*above*), marlin, and tuna also have eye-warming organs like swordfish.

A Growing Swordfish

Swordfish spend most of their lives alone in the open ocean. This area is also known as the pelagic zone.

In warm areas of the ocean, swordfish meet to **spawn** throughout the year. But in colder areas, spawning occurs only in the spring and summer months.

FAST FACTS Unlike adult swordfish, young swordfish have both scales and teeth.

Swordfish are usually solitary creatures. Male and female swordfish only meet to spawn.

Swordfish are less than one-quarter inch (.64 cm) long when they hatch. They live at the surface of the ocean and feed on **plankton**. Some are eaten by other plankton eaters.

Swordfish go through many changes on the way to adulthood. There are at least six different stages!

Swordfish Growth Stages

A Small Family

Swordfish are the only known member of their family. They do not have any close relatives.

However, there are other fish in the sea with swords or saws. These include marlins, sailfish, sawfish, and sawsharks.

A sawshark has a long, pointed snout lined with teeth like a saw. And barbels dangle on each side of the snout. These barbels act as feelers and help the shark find prey on the sandy ocean floor.

Marlins grow very large. The largest are about 16 feet (5 m) long. They can weigh up to 1,500 pounds (680 kg)!

Sawfish are related to sharks and rays. They can be as small as five feet (2 m). But most are much larger. The largest sawfish grow to about 20 feet (6 m). Some weigh more than 5,000 pounds (2,300 kg)!

Sailfish are named for the collapsible sail on their backs. These fish are the fastest in the ocean! They can move more than 68 miles (109 km) per hour!

The Lone Fish

Swordfish are **solitary** creatures. They do not swim in schools.

The open ocean is their home. They move around often. Their neighbors change depending on where they are.

At times, the open ocean can seem as empty as a desert canyon. But, empty areas can suddenly fill with life. This happens when ocean **currents** meet or **spawning** seasons arrive.

Swordfish, dolphins, tuna, and other predators seek out these large gatherings of fish. They may travel great distances each year to visit these highly populated areas.

Like swordfish, sharks hunt large schools of fish. These fish have formed a tight ball in defense.

Night Hunters

Swordfish are **carnivores**. They feed on squid, octopuses, and many kinds of fish. They use their sharp bills to slash at schools of fish and squid. Swordfish then eat the wounded animals.

Swordfish eat squid *(above)*, octopuses *(right)*, and butterfly fish *(below)*.

Scientists say swordfish hunt every night near the ocean's surface. Many other ocean animals also go to the surface each night. So, it is a good place for predators to hunt. This daily upward movement is called vertical migration.

FAST FACTS

During World War II, U.S. submarine operators saw the vertical migrations of many animals on sonar screens. These animals produced a strong sonar echo. The U.S. Navy used this echo to hide!

Moon jellies migrate to the ocean surface daily.
There, they catch the day's last rays of sun.

Danger, Danger!

The world is a dangerous place for swordfish. Sharks such as the fast-swimming mako eat adult swordfish. So do killer whales and sperm whales. Fish such as dolphinfish, yellowfin tuna, and marlins eat young swordfish.

Humans are the swordfish's most dangerous enemy. People catch swordfish for both sport and food. Experts say many young swordfish have been taken from the ocean. Because of this, fewer swordfish reach adult size.

The National Marine Fisheries Service reports the average swordfish weight has dropped. In 1960, it was 260 pounds (120 kg). In 1996, it was only 90 pounds (40 kg).

Swordfish fishing is popular among sport fishermen.

Fascinating Facts

Remoras are also called suckerfish. They use suction to attach themselves to other fish.

Remora's Sucker

🗡 Swordfish are great jumpers. They are often seen jumping above the ocean's surface. Some scientists believe they do this to remove **parasites**, such as lampreys or remoras.

🗡 Swordfish are fast! They can swim up to 60 miles (97 km) per hour.

It is easy for fishermen in large boats to harpoon swordfish. The swordfish seem to avoid small boats. But, they seem drawn to large ones!

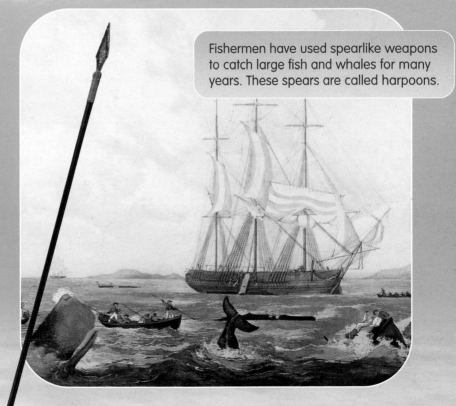

Fishermen have used spearlike weapons to catch large fish and whales for many years. These spears are called harpoons.

Learn And Explore

Scientists say that eating swordfish may be harmful to human health.

A chemical called methyl mercury has gotten into much of the world's water. It comes from manufacturing processes and burning coal. And, it is toxic to humans.

Swordfish flesh has particularly high levels of this **toxin**. So, experts say people should limit the amount of swordfish they eat. This is especially true for children.

IMPORTANT WORDS

carnivore a meat-eater.

current the flow and movement of a large body of water.

invertebrate an animal without a backbone.

parasite an animal that lives on or in another animal and gets food without giving anything back.

solitary alone.

spawn to reproduce.

species living things that are very much alike.

temperate an area on Earth where temperatures are mild.

toxin a harmful substance.

tropical an area on Earth where temperatures are warm.

WEB SITES

To learn more about the swordfish, visit ABDO Publishing Company on the World Wide Web. Web sites about swordfish are featured on our Book Links page. These links are routinely monitored and updated to provide the most current information available.

www.abdopublishing.com

INDEX